Spanish Alphabet
Coloring Book

Nina Barbaresi

Dover Publications, Inc., New York

Preface

THIS BOOK IS DESIGNED to help children learn the Spanish alphabet and over 150 Spanish words while they enjoy coloring the illustrations. Each page is devoted to one letter of the alphabet and contains various Spanish words beginning with that letter. At the bottom of each page is an alphabetical list of all the words appearing on that page. This list provides the English equivalents for the Spanish words along with their definite articles (English "the"). In Spanish, there are two gender-indicating definite articles in the singular: *el* (for masculine nouns) and *la* (for feminine nouns). To indicate the plural, the mas-culine article is *los*, and the feminine article is *las*. There is, however, one important exception to the rule governing the use of the definite article in the singular. To make pronunciation easier, feminine nouns beginning with a stressed "a" sound (this occurs in some words beginning with the letter "a" and some beginning "ha") the mas-culine article *el* is used. Thus, the feminine noun *águila* (eagle) appears as *el águila* (the eagle). Since the gender of such nouns is not imme-diately obvious, the abbreviation F (for feminine) has been given with such words.

Published in Canada by General Publishing Company, Ltd., 30 Lesmill Road, Don Mills, Toronto, Ontario.
Published in the United Kingdom by Constable and Company, Ltd., 3 The Lanchesters, 162–164 Fulham Palace Road, London W6 9ER.

Spanish Alphabet Coloring Book is a new work, first published by Dover Publications, Inc., in 1992.

International Standard Book Number: 0-486-27249-4

Manufactured in the United States of America
Dover Publications, Inc., 31 East 2nd Street, Mineola, N.Y. 11501

árbol

avión

abeja

araña

ardilla

águila

la abeja (the bee); el águila (F., the eagle); la araña (the spider); el árbol (the tree); la ardilla (the squirrel); el avión (the airplane)

3

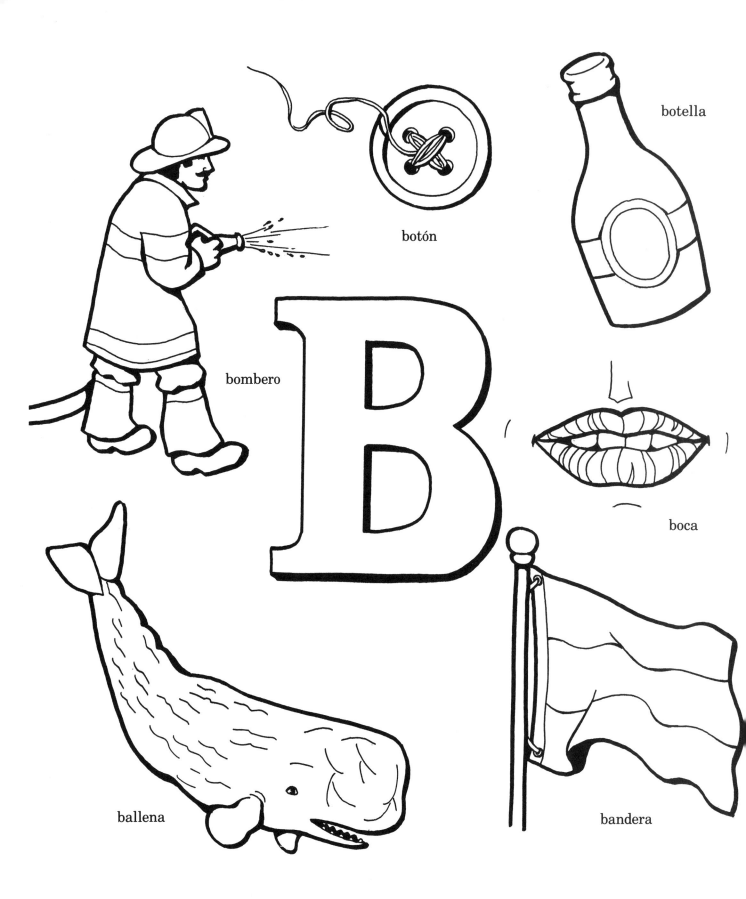

botella

botón

bombero

B

boca

ballena

bandera

la ballena (the whale); la bandera (the flag); la boca (the mouth); el bombero (the fireman); la botella (the bottle); el botón (the button)

caballo

cama

cabeza

cuchara

casa

camisa

el caballo (the horse); la cabeza (the head); la cama (the bed); la
camisa (the shirt); la casa (the house); la cuchara (the spoon)

chacal

chiles

chaqueta

Ch

chimpancé

chivo

chinchilla

el chacal (the jackal); la chaqueta (the jacket); los chiles (the chilis); el chimpancé (the chimpanzee); la chinchilla (the chinchilla); el chivo (the kid, the goat)

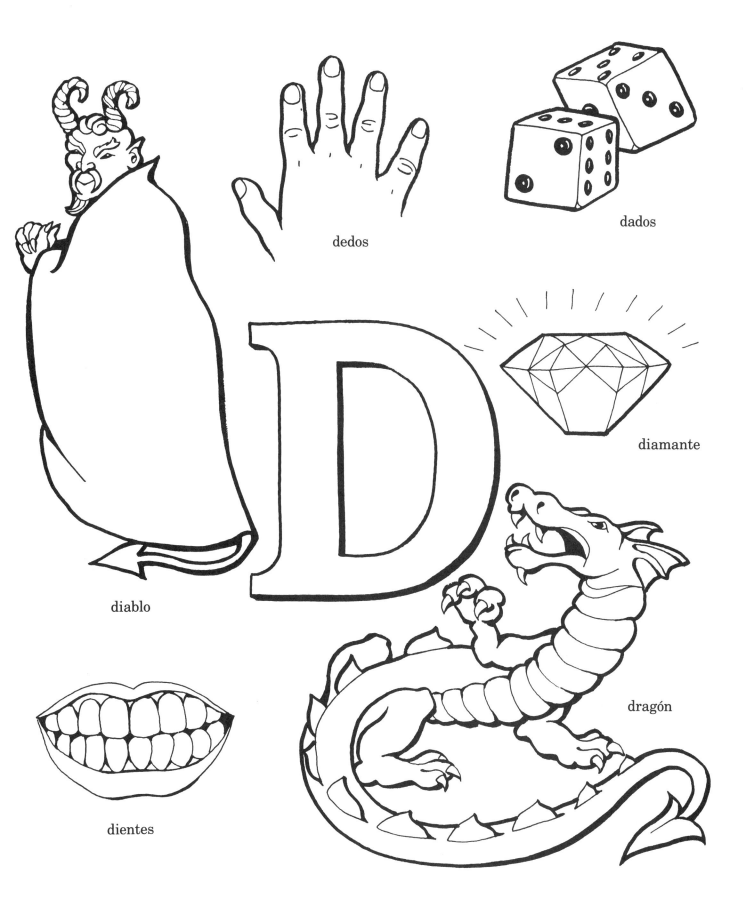

dedos

dados

diamante

diablo

dragón

dientes

los dados (the dice); los dedos (the fingers); el diablo (the devil);
el diamante (the diamond); los dientes (the teeth); el dragón
(the dragon)

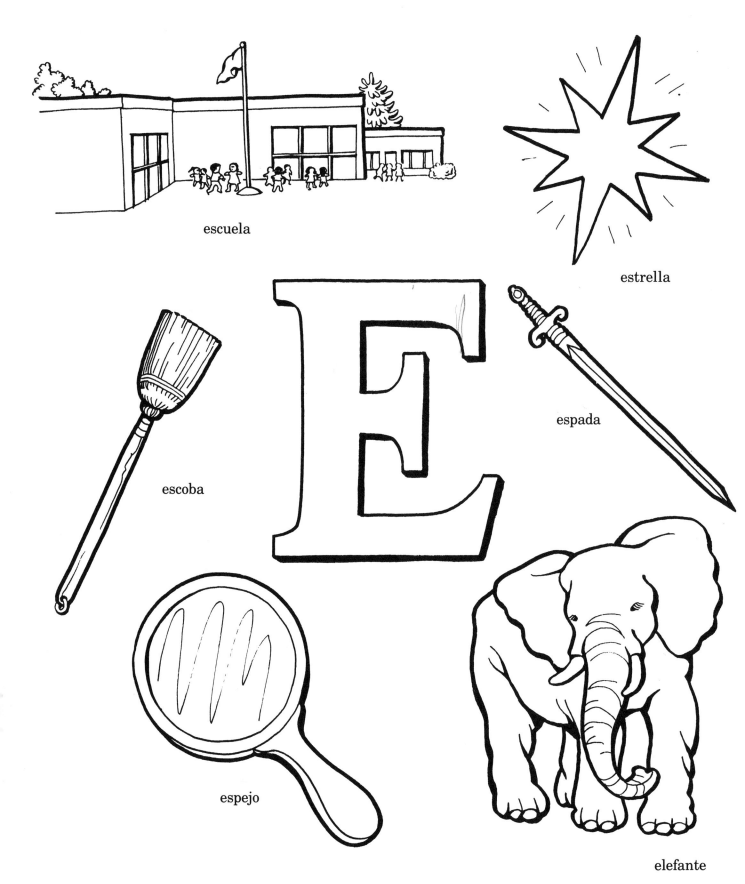

escuela

estrella

escoba

espada

espejo

elefante

el elefante (the elephant); la escoba (the broom); la escuela (the school); la espada (the sword); el espejo (the mirror); la estrella (the star)

flecha

fresas

flores

fuego

flamenco

falda

la falda (the skirt); el flamenco (the flamingo); la flecha (the arrow); las flores (the flowers); las fresas (the strawberries); el fuego (the fire)

globo

gallo

guitarra

guantes

gato

gaviota

el gallo (the cock); el gato (the cat); la gaviota (the seagull); el globo (the balloon); los guantes (the gloves); la guitarra (the guitar)

hombre

helado

hormiga

hongo

hoja

hada

el hada (F., the fairy); el helado (the ice cream); la hoja (the leaf); el hombre (the man); el hongo (the mushroom); la hormiga (the ant)

iglú

iguana

imán

I

isla

iglesia

insecto

la iglesia (the church); el iglú (the igloo); la iguana (the iguana);
el imán (the magnet); el insecto (the insect); la isla (the island)

joyas

jirafa

jamón

jardín

juguetes

jabón

el jabón (the soap); el jamón (the ham); el jardín (the garden); la jirafa (the giraffe); las joyas (the jewels); los juguetes (the toys)

kilt

kiwi

koala

K

karate

kimono

kayac

el karate (karate); el kayac (the kayak); el kilt (the kilt); el
kimono (the kimono); el kiwi (the kiwi); el koala (the koala)

luna

león

libro

labios

lagarto

lobo

los labios (the lips); el lagarto (the lizard); el león (the lion); el libro (the book); el lobo (the wolf); la luna (the moon)

lluvia

llave

llama

la llama (the llama); la llave (the key); la lluvia (the rain)

mano

manzana

mariposa

mujer

médico

mesa

la mano (the hand); la manzana (the apple); la mariposa (the butterfly); el médico (the doctor); la mesa (the table); la mujer (the woman)

nido

nieve

nariz

navío

niños

nudo

la nariz (the nose); el navío (the ship); el nido (the nest); la nieve
(the snow); los niños (the children); el nudo (the knot)

ñame

ñandú

ñu

el ñame (the yam); el ñandú (the nandu, American ostrich); el
ñu (the gnu)

ojo

olla

oveja

oreja

oso

oruga

el ojo (the eye); la olla (the pot); la oreja (the ear); la oruga (the caterpillar); el oso (the bear); la oveja (the sheep)

pan

pantalones

paraguas

pájaro

perro

puerta

el pájaro (the bird); el pan (the bread); los pantalones (the trousers); el paraguas (the umbrella); el perro (the dog); la puerta (the door)

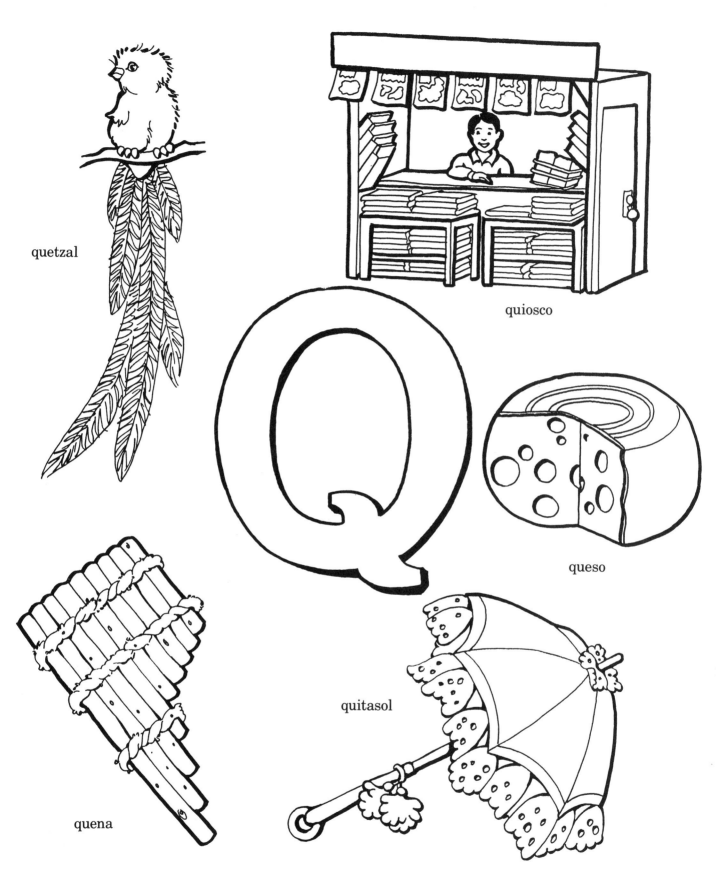

quetzal

quiosco

queso

quitasol

quena

la quena (the quena, Indian flute); el queso (the cheese); el quetzal (the quetzal); el quiosco (the kiosk); el quitasol (the parasol)

ratón

reloj

rosa

R

rana

rey

reina

la rana (the frog); el ratón (the mouse); la reina (the queen); el
reloj (the watch); el rey (the king); la rosa (the rose)

23

sirena

sol

soldado

silla

sombra

sombrero

la silla (the chair); la sirena (the mermaid); el sol (the sun); el soldado (the soldier); la sombra (the shadow); el sombrero (the hat)

24

tenedor

toro

tren

taza

teléfono

tigre

la taza (the cup); el teléfono (the telephone); el tenedor (the fork); el tigre (the tiger); el toro (the bull); el tren (the train)

ukelele

uña

unicornio

U

uvas

urubú

el ukelele (the ukulele); el unicornio (the unicorn); la uña (the fingernail); el urubú (the urubu, black vulture); las uvas (the grapes)

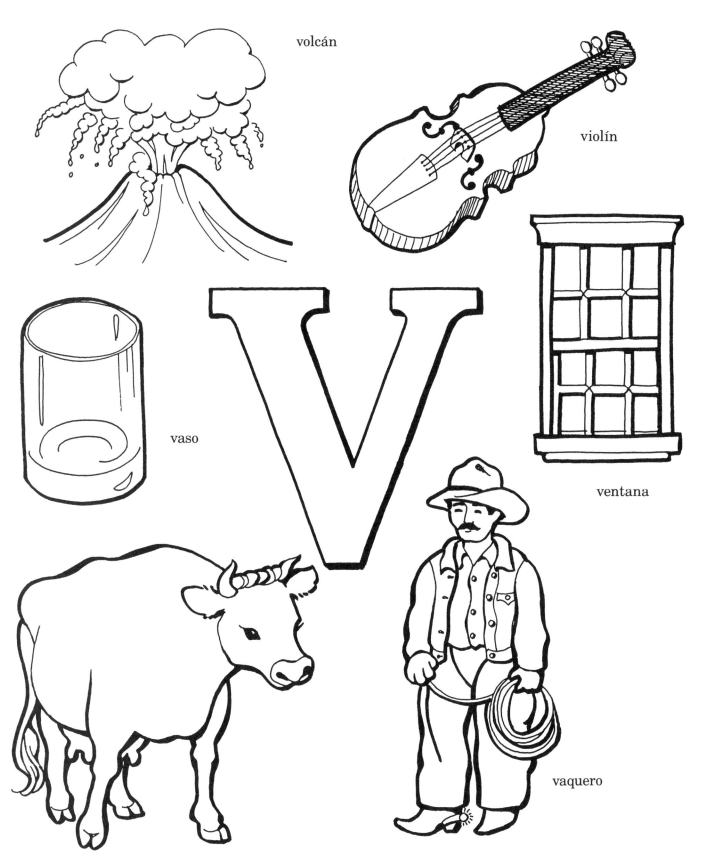

volcán

violín

ventana

vaso

vaca

vaquero

la vaca (the cow); el vaquero (the cowboy); el vaso (the drinking glass); la ventana (the window); el violín (the violin); el volcán (the volcano)

western

water-polo

wharf

wapití

el wapití (the wapiti); el water-polo (water polo); el western (the western film); el wharf (the wharf)

xilografía

X

xilófono

el xilófono (the xylophone); la xilografía (the wood engraving)

yugo

yac

Y

yunque

yoyo

yate

el yac (the yak); el yate (the yacht); el yoyo (the yo-yo); el yugo
(the yoke); el yunque (the anvil)

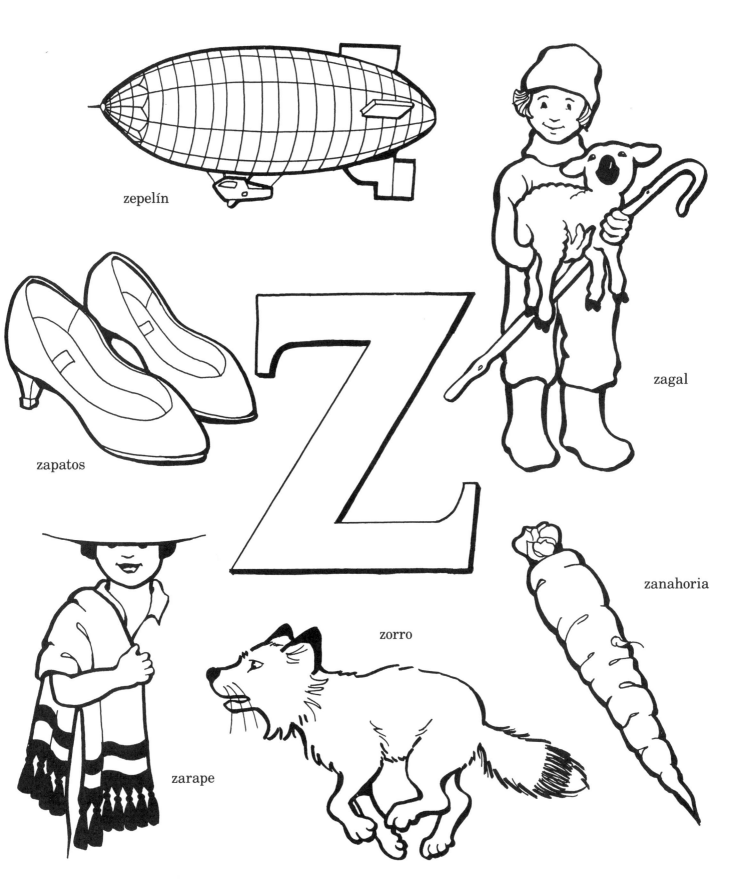

zepelín

zapatos

zagal

zanahoria

zorro

zarape

el zagal (the shepherd boy); la zanahoria (the carrot); los zapatos (the shoes); el zarape (the serape); el zepelín (the zeppelin); el zorro (the fox)